ANCIENT WORLD

A CHAPTER BOOK

BY KATHERINE GLEASON

15442

children's press®

A Division of Scholastic Inc.

New York   Toronto   London   Auckland   Sydney
Mexico City   New Delhi   Hong Kong
Danbury, Connecticut

In memory of Mark Dallas Butler (1961–1993)

ACKNOWLEDGMENTS

The author would like to thank all the archeologists whose exciting work
and patience in answering questions made this book possible. In particular, thanks
and best wishes go to Dr. William A. Saturno, Director, Proyecto San Bartolo,
La Antigua, Guatemala; Dr. Winifred Creamer, Professor of Anthropology,
Northern Illinois University, DeKalb, Illinois; Dr. Jonathan Haas, Curator,
Field Museum, Chicago, Illinois; Dr. Rick Jones, Project Director, Anglo-American
Project in Pompeii and Reader in Roman Archaeological Sciences,
University of Bradford, Bradford, United Kingdom; Astrid Schoonhoven

Library of Congress Cataloging-in-Publication Data

Gleason, Katherine.
  Ancient world : a chapter book / by Katherine Gleason.
    p. cm. – (True tales)
Includes bibliographical references and index.
Contents: The valley of the mummies – An amazing mural – The oldest
city in the Americas – Ancient meals.
  ISBN 0-516-22916-8 (lib. bdg.)   0-516-24600-3 (pbk.)
  1. Civilization, Ancient–Juvenile literature. [1. Civilization,
Ancient.] I. Title. II. Series.
  CB311.G54 2003
                     2003004446

© 2003 Nancy Hall, Inc.
Published in 2003 by Children's Press
A Division of Scholastic Inc.

1 2 3 4 5 6 7 8 9 10 R 12 11 10 09 08 07 06 05 04 03

CONTENTS

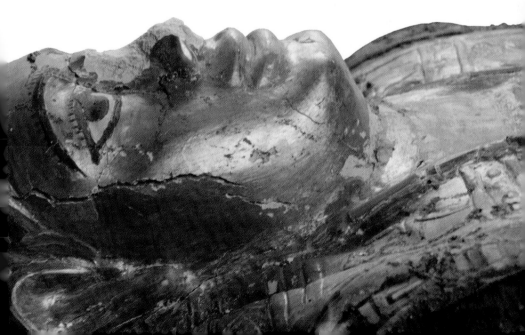

INTRODUCTION

Long ago, the world was different from the way it is now. There were no cars, no computers, and no television in **ancient** (AYN-shunt) times. In this book, you'll meet people who study life in the ancient world. To discover what life was like back then, they dig up old cities.

Doctor Zahi Hawass uncovered an exciting discovery in a desert in Egypt. Doctor William Saturno traveled far into the rain forest. While there, he discovered something that surprised him. Doctor Ruth Shady Solis and a team of scientists (SYE-uhn-tiss) discovered that a city in Peru is the oldest city in the Americas. Doctor Rick Jones looks so carefully at one ancient city he even knows what the people ate.

Read about these amazing discoveries and learn about the people who dig up the past.

CHAPTER ONE

VALLEY OF THE MUMMIES

In 1996, Aiad was riding his donkey to work. Aiad worked as a guard in Egypt, a country in Africa. Somewhere in the desert, the donkey tripped and fell. The donkey's leg was caught in a hole in the ground. Aiad looked into the hole. He saw gold. Aiad hurried to tell his boss. His boss hurried to tell Doctor Zahi Hawass.

Zahi is an **archeologist** (ar-kee-OL-uh-jist). He studies what people were like long ago. Zahi and his team started to dig near the hole. They dug up four underground rooms where dead people are buried. These rooms are called **tombs** (TOOMS). The archeologists found 105 **mummies** inside the tombs.

Doctor Zahi Hawass

A mummy is a dead body that has been treated to make it last for a long time. The ancient Egyptians made mummies by taking out the body's inner **organs**. Then they dried the body. They covered it with oil and wrapped it in cloth.

The mummies Zahi found are about 2,000 years old. Some of the mummies are covered with a layer of gold. Some lie in

A layer of gold covers some of the mummies.

Some of the mummies have pictures painted on their body.

boxes made of clay. Each of these boxes, or **coffins**, is painted with a human face. Other mummies are wrapped in cloth. Other mummies wear a mask. These mummies have pictures painted on their body. The pictures show the **gods** and **goddesses** of Egypt.

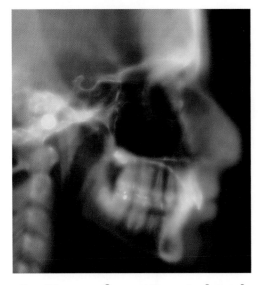

An X ray of a person's head

Zahi took **X rays** of one mummy. He learned that the mummy had been a young man when he died. The man had not been sick before he died. What had caused the man's death?

The archeologists wanted to find the answer. They took X rays of other mummies. Many of the mummies were of people who had died young. They also had not been sick before they died.

Scientists did tests. They learned that the bones of the mummies had too much iron. The iron came from the drinking water. Most likely, the people had died after drinking too much of this water.

An archeologist studying mummies

Zahi and his team have dug up more than 230 mummies. There may be as many as 10,000 mummies in the area. This is more mummies than have ever been found in one place. Today, the place is known as the Valley of the Mummies.

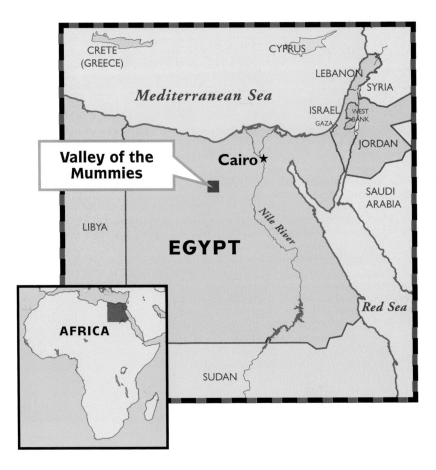

CHAPTER TWO

A MAYA MURAL

One day in 2001, Doctor William Saturno traveled into the rain forest of Guatemala (gwah-tuh-MAH-luh). He was looking for some special stones. He did not find any. Instead, he found something much more unusual.

A Maya pyramid

A rain forest

William traveled for three days. In the middle of the forest he found a **ruin** (ROO-in). He named it San Bartolo.

William did not know the trip would take so long. By the second day, he had used up all his food and water. He was hungry, thirsty, and hot. To get out of the sun, he climbed into a tunnel near a **pyramid** (PIHR-uh-mid).

William Saturno studies a mural in San Bartolo.

William rested in the shade. Then, he turned on his flashlight. He let the light shine on the walls of the tunnel. A huge painting was on one wall. William was amazed. He had just discovered an ancient **mural**. "I felt like the luckiest man on the planet," he said.

William is an **archeologist** who studies the **Maya** (MYE-uh). The ancient Maya were people who lived in Mexico and Central America a very long time ago.

Around 2000 B.C., the Maya began to build small towns. They went on to build cities, palaces, roads, and courts where they

A Maya palace

Maya hieroglyphs

played ball. They invented a type of writing known as **hieroglyphs** (hye-ur-uh-GLIFS). They carved these hieroglyphs into stone and painted them on walls and vases.

The Maya also knew math. They were some of the first people to invent a way to count large numbers. They understood how the sun and the moon moved. They even figured out that a year is made up of 365 days. The Maya were some of the most advanced people of the ancient world.

Maya calendar

In 2001, a team of archeologists went to see the mural. The mural is about 1,900 years old. It is the oldest Maya mural ever found. The mural is painted on a wall that used to be part of a room. The room is full of pieces of broken stone and dirt.

One part of the mural

An artist's drawing of how the mural looked

Archeologists need to dig more stone and dirt out of the room. Then they will be able to see the whole mural. The part they can see is about 6 feet (1.8 meters) long and 2 feet (0.6 meters) high.

This part of the mural shows a group of people. Some of them are kneeling. The mural also shows a man. The man is standing. He is looking over his shoulder at two women. Who is this man? Archeologists think that he is the Maya corn god. The ancient king at San Bartolo probably asked the painter of the mural to paint this god. The painting probably honors the king and his power.

Maya corn god

An artist is working with the archeologists. She is copying the mural. She uses a camera and

21

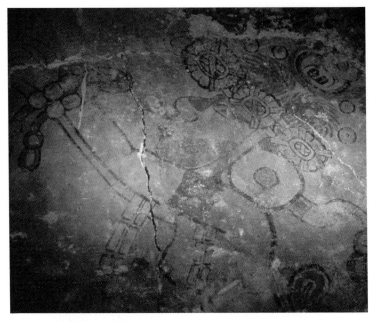

The paint of the mural is faded.

a computer to help her. A photographer is taking pictures of the mural. People all over the world can look at the photographs and drawings. This way they can study the mural, too. The pictures are also important in case the mural gets ruined. If that happens, archeologists will still have a record of what the mural looked like.

The archeologists are digging to uncover more of the mural. They are working to save the mural, too. The wall under the

Archeologists look at a piece of the mural.

mural was removed. The archeologists are using pieces of wood to hold up the mural. Then they will build a new wall.

The archeologists will keep working at San Bartolo. They want to find out everything they can about the mural. They know that the mural will help them learn even more about the ancient Maya.

William (right) looks at the walls of a pyramid.

CHAPTER THREE

THE OLDEST CITY IN THE AMERICAS

In the center of Caral, Peru, are six huge stone buildings. These buildings are called **platform mounds**. They are flat on the top. The biggest mound is 60 feet (18 meters) high and 500 feet (152 meters) long.

Doctor Ruth Shady Solis and a team of **archeologists** dug into the base of a mound.

The biggest mound is 60 feet (18 meters) high and 50 feet (152 meters) long.

They looked inside the wall of the mound. They found bags inside. The bags are made of **reeds**. The archeologists think that workers used these reed bags when they built the mounds. Hundreds of workers carried stones in them.

Caral is very dry. Because it is so dry, the reed bags did not decay. The archeologists took one of the bags to a lab. Scientists at

Archeologists think that workers used bags made of reed to carry stones.

the lab did tests. They found that the bags were about 4,600 years old. This is how the archeologists learned that the mounds were built between 2627 and 2000 B.C. They are about the same age as the pyramids of Egypt.

This makes Caral the oldest city in the Americas. Caral is more than 1,000 years older than any other American city. This ancient city lies in a valley. It is about 14 miles (22.5 kilometers) from the Pacific

Ocean. It is 125 miles (201 kilometers) north of Lima, the capital city of Peru.

Archeologists first visited Caral in 1905. Many of these archeologists did not find Caral interesting. Because the platform mounds were so large, they thought Caral could not be very old. They thought that ancient workers did not have the skill to make such big structures.

Caral is the oldest city in the Americas.

There was another reason archeologists paid little attention to Caral. The ancient people who lived there did not grow corn. In the past, archeologists thought unless ancient people knew how to grow corn, they could not be very successful. Corn was important to ancient people because it can be kept for a long time. Because of this, ancient people used corn like money. Workers were paid with corn. No one is sure how the workers of Caral were paid. They may have been paid with dried fish.

The people of Caral ate fish. They also grew squash, beans, and other vegetables (VEG-tuh-buhls) for food. They watered

A furnace

their crops with an **irrigation system**. Caral
may have been the first American city to
bring in water this way.

Archeologists also found furnaces.
Ancient people used the furnaces for many
purposes. They cooked in them. They also
sat near them to keep warm.

The archeologists will continue to study
the platform mounds at Caral. They will

also keep digging so they can learn more. They want to know what is inside the mounds. There may be rooms inside. Maybe people lived in the mounds. Maybe they kept things inside the mounds. There may be tombs inside. Anything that the archeologists find will help them learn more about Caral. They want to understand everything about the Americas' oldest city.

CHAPTER FOUR

ANCIENT MEALS

On August 24, A.D. 79, a **volcano** near
Pompeii **erupted**. It threw ash on the city.
Houses, people, and even dogs were buried.
Before the volcano exploded, Pompeii had
been a busy city. About 20,000 people lived
there. The city was full of houses, shops,
and factories.

The town of Pompeii today

**Houses, people, and even dogs
were covered in ash.**

Today, Pompeii is home to a big
archeological dig. There is even a school
of **archeology** (ar-kee-OL-uh-jee) there. In
the summer, college students come
from many countries to learn to be
archeologists.
Doctor Rick Jones is an archeologist
who teaches at the school. Every
summer, he leads a team of
students to study Pompeii.

Doctor Rick Jones

Students discover what life in Pompeii was like.

This is what Pompeii looks like.

The students discover what life in Pompeii was like. They learn about the houses in Pompeii. They learn where the people worked. They even learn what the people of the city ate.

eggshells

They learn about the food by digging up ancient kitchens. In the kitchen of a rich person, they uncovered different kinds of food. To find the foods, they sifted dirt by pushing it through a screen. Tiny pieces of pepper were in the dirt.

Rick and his students found eggshells, too. They found fish scales and shells from seafood. One student even found an ancient tooth.

fish bones

fish scales

These paintings show different kinds of food eaten in Pompeii.

Paintings in the house show some other kinds of food. The paintings show a chicken, a goose, a goat, some fish, and a rabbit. The people in this house probably ate these things. They even ate tiny birds called sparrows. They ate different kinds of cheeses and vegetables, too. For dessert, they ate fruit, such as figs and apricots.

Outside the house, Rick and his students found six fish tanks. The people in the house may have sold fresh fish. The fish may also have been used to make **garum** (GAR-uhm), a spicy sauce. The people of Pompeii made garum by putting fish in salt water. They left the fish to rot. After a few days, they would have a smelly, salty sauce to put over food. The people in the house may have made garum and sold it to make money.

Rick found a fish skeleton (SKEL-uh-tuhn) inside a fish tank. The skeleton is from a small fish. The archeologists are studying the fish skeleton. They want to know all about life in ancient Pompeii.

GLOSSARY

ancient (AYN-shunt) from a long time ago; very old

archeologist (ar-kee-OL-uh-jist) someone who studies the way people lived a long time ago

archeology (ar-kee-OL-uh-jee) the study of the way people lived a long time ago

coffin a box used to bury a dead person

erupt what a volcano does when it throws out lava, ash, and gas

garum (GAR-uhm) a sauce made from fish and salt

god a being with special powers who is worshipped

goddess a female god

hieroglyph (hye-ur-uh-GLIF) a picture or symbol used in ancient writing

irrigation system a network of pipes and ditches that bring water to dry land

Maya (MYE-uh) a people of Mexico and Central America

mummy the body of a dead person that has been dried and saved

mural a painting done on a wall

organ a part of the body that does a certain job

platform mound a large ancient building with a flat top made from stones and dirt

pyramid (PIHR-uh-mid) an ancient stone building where people are buried

reed a kind of grass that grows near water

ruin (ROO-in) what is left after something has been destroyed

tomb (TOOM) an underground room for the dead

volcano a mountain with a tube in the center through which lava, ash, and gas erupt

X ray a kind of picture that shows the bones inside a body

FIND OUT MORE

Valley of the Mummies
www.guardians.net/hawass/index.htm
See pictures and read more about Doctor Hawass and his work.

A Maya Mural
www.sanbartolo.org
Follow the on-going research on an ancient Maya mural.

The Oldest City in the Americas
www.sciencenews.org/20010428/fob1.asp
Learn about Caral, Peru.

Ancient Meals
http://www.cs.berkeley.edu/~jhauser/pictures/history/Romans/Pompeii
See how the ancient city of Pompeii looks today.

More Books to Read

Secrets in Stone: All About Maya Hieroglyphics by Laurie Coulter, Little Brown & Company, 2001

Peru by Elaine Landau, Children's Press, 2000

Eyewitness: Mummy by James Putnam, DK Publishing, 2000

The Buried City of Pompeii: What It Was Like When Vesuvius Exploded by Shelley Tanaka, Hyperion Press, 2000

INDEX

PHOTO CREDITS

MEET THE AUTHOR

Katherine Gleason has worked in children's publishing as an editor, project manager, and author. She has written numerous books for children and a few for adults, as well. She particularly enjoys writing and reading books about ancient cultures and faraway places. Her love of travel has taken her all over the world, and she has, in fact, visited all seven of the Earth's continents. Gleason lives in New York City with her cat, Elphaba.